the
little
edges

wesleyan poetry

Also by Fred Moten

POETRY

The Feel Trio

B Jenkins

Hughson's Tavern

I ran from it and was still in it.
    (with collages by Theodore Harris)

Poems (with Jim Behrle)

Arkansas

NONFICTION

In the Break: The Aesthetics of the Black Radical Tradition

The Undercommons: Fugitive Planning and Black Study
    (with Stefano Harney)

Fred Moten

the little edges

wesleyan university press | middletown, connecticut

Wesleyan University Press
Middletown CT 06459
www.wesleyan.edu/wespress
© 2015 Frederick Moten
All rights reserved
Manufactured in the United States of America
Designed and typeset in Fresco Plus Pro
and DIN Next Pro by Eric M. Brooks

Wesleyan University Press is a member of
the Green Press Initiative. The paper used in
this book meets their minimum requirement
for recycled paper.

ART WORKS.
arts.gov

*This project is supported in part by an award
from the National Endowment for the Arts.*

Library of Congress
Cataloging-in-Publication Data
Moten, Fred.
[Poems. Selections]
The little edges / Fred Moten.
pages; cm — (Wesleyan poetry series)
ISBN 978-0-8195-7505-0 (cloth: alk. paper) —
ISBN 978-0-8195-7506-7 (ebook)
I. Title.
PS3563.O8867A6   2014
811'.54 — dc23   2014018094

5 4 3 2 1

to frequent,
to gather,
to solemnize in joy,
to enjoy,
to sing praise,
to practice,
to assemble in disassembly,
to be quietly populous,
to publish intimately,
to repeat this often,
to josé esteban muñoz,
originally of the mass.

contents

the
little
edges

fortrd.fortrn

that's what rodney asked about,
can you make what we already (do
you remember/how did the people)

have? let it get around and get on in

                        complicity,
                        in scar city,
ar.   complexcity

        in complicita, la.   here go a box with a lid on it. if you open it you can come into our world.

                        up in here you look

                        like cutty do. house
                        look like he up. if so,

                        don't you wanna go?

live, remote, preoccupied
with breathing and black
as machine ecology, iron
man, all over the pan, all over the basin,

duone, chant carry pauses and actually live inside 'em, gift
double, to see things and say can hear them vary, pearl,
from then beginning all gone inside, remember, threshold,
surround her separateness with bands but if I were a bell?

exhaustion makes life ever
lasting. when I dance with

you I am the moved mover.

baby, you're a solid sender.

we pound plenty, baby, softened in our program, our transubstantial fade and crossfade bodies, baby.

take this and think about

me in the first place. begin
in the real presence of my

skin, baby. you shook me!

your hand is my pocket.

I'm a pocket man. your
hand is in my pocket. I
fix broken rockets. you

are my starship. you're

all I need. you send for

me and I can't keep my
self from coming, baby,

as I am, I have what I already have, I'm yours.

precision and humility in the experiment
is written on the way you customize your

uniform, a ritual of lotion and stillness in
the morning, 'fore you make it in to work

on the

edge of
   your
train

on the edge because you're driven to the edge in your violent correctness,

over the edge of what you're listening to like somebody listening to you.

you might
   be one.

you might be someone that needs listening to. you might need somebody, too.
a lot of this is found in what we have. almost all of this belongs to you. are you
gon' gimme some? naw, you on your way to work,

little sister. that's alright, young man. bye, baby.

the unspeakable tower is what they did.
our shit has some names and sometimes
they sound good at the bottom of it, therefore proceed
against that little pill-head fucker that correct people's pronunciation.

fotrad.fotran ain't really got to where we got somewhere to go,

premature precepts dripped from deferred foreskins,

brought out from nowhere with forecepts with no receptacle,
but early on my grammar cleft my palette with okras

and blues. mimi said don't listen to them blues.

she knew she should because her shoe moved. she knew
the man playing ray charles was ray charles. she put the jazz-cri
on an early stove, cooked it down to a low gravy,

(with this trade, these little fours, your dirty palette, a savory train between in blood sorbet)

let it dry and made a vase out of it. we poured what was in it
on our greens and blues and ochres, our loud flavors
and the tree we danced around, the tree we made a movie around,
against that little pill-head fucker that correct people's predestination.

fo fo fo
four four four

fore fore fore
foe foe foe

semper fe, semper fi, motherfucker,

fume instead of kill. the incident in
crosshatch is a burst of whispers. a

mouthpiece and burred air. in need
turned out to be our desire. a video

of the archive in play. it's some indelicate

news on the wall. something in silence for
everything that everybody ever wanted. cri
sis for everything that ever burned inside.

my baby's black representational space is another world.

black workers of the other world unite up in there, one
named peanut the other named bush, making shit up in

chance theater, which is a truck farm in exploded rows.

my baby's black representational space is the south
dakota hills. you like the comfortable surprise of its
location? see how it travels? it's other than itself and

it sells itself that way. whose little self are you? mine.

my baby's black representational space is all over the

place so he got to move his body. body cut the neuro

typical field with a razor in the shape of a basketball.
somebody sing give me body you can hear it bounce.

my baby's black representational space is a black head on

some black skin. in the city of the blemish on the blemish
of delivery the mayor's name is da mayor; but you can call
her woody or few or mole in the ground or at your service.

hand up to your ear

(for you to find a way to sound and move, dont rhymes with robert's selmer like a plastic fuse, to blow out the emperor's

ambience with shouting in the theological desert of the city. you bring with you to galleries an echo of shipping, an avenue

warehouse, a river bea, and the prendergast machine is discipline against an echo of shopping, too much arrangement in

the head, susan's sound through store-bought power. that show of shows is a bill of lading, a business pleasure, and the
auctioneer's nervous run is overtaken by worn shadow, homeless ware is walking, the armory is walking away, some nervous

agent in the air)

Dont Rhine and Robert Sember 1.24.12/3.29.12
CAConrad, Amiri Baraka, Angela Davis, M. NourbeSe Philip 4.16-20.12

laurie prendergast and Susan Jahoda (diving) 5.5.12

You are a base community

Apprehend before the sound. The cargo, the brutalized openings, which also surround it, but only for a time that can't be measured, in permeance. It's an imprecision bordering on invasion to call this context, that

rapturous silence, shouting, composed in listening so we discompose ourselves in one another. Lose your

composure in repose, at rest, in descent, in the general murmur, a general antagonism of noise, the fugue of the absolutely poor, her gift of diving, her depressive largesse of lifting, in study, in series, her overlapped

happenings of attendance, lapsed concentricities, submerged cyphers, like a bunch of little churches and ballrooms with open doors.

You are the bottom

We care about each other so militantly, with such softness, that we exhaust ourselves, and then record, in the resonance of our slightly opened mouths, the sound of that, in the absence of the enemy that we keep making.

A disconnected movement, as if preoccupied, held already in the beautiful gathering afternoon, carried by one

another as one another's play mamas. Listen to the sound through one another's skin. Preserve the sound through membrane and water, to find our form in corresponding.

Your body is a mixing board

Come take a listening walk and admire your hand twisting. The listening is in watching how you move to

touch in sounding, brushing up against your friend, to see how his position sounds to make the music we are making by moving the people moving around. Make soundworks out of rustling to notice the material that

comes up on us, that we come upon, do something with. Do something with the sound like it's your friend,

like you met her at the quadrophenic playground.

You are a child, in a club

One night in San Francisco, off the impeccable to fray nailed stud of a live black hawk, of the more and less than full divided air of a mystophone, through her diviséd air, o master of ceremonies miles, like a speaker in a whisper with a monster, say form a pit and brush somebody hand. Make a mix in violent rubbing till your work is gone. Make a prompt a foursquare then the squares collapse as separates but other than before till work is made to disappear to register its fields as present in the sound and its sources. Everybody brush somebody hand till work is gone to the alternate slam. How long can you sustain the foursquare? This is how to make little works just walking down the street, collaborating with the hand you brush, as shawls serrate the length of her arcade.

You want sensory issues

Curate the sound you make by jumping. Flap your hands before your eyes. In lengthening, become from another country. Imitate the movement but expel more air. Say this is your house and run a lap in it but dance

with the air immediately around the ones who seem at home. Repeat a word or phrase, slightly louder, up

three steps then down, like a color block in a Hoffman painting. For a minute say every letter of every word

but slowly. Hold somebody hand up to your ear.

hard enough to enjoy

Ralph Lemon was born in Cincinnati, Ohio. Queen Records' infant archivist and rhythmicon, his contributions to the theory of gravity, a flowncrawled chorograph of attractions breathing the variously collided particles of isley, collins, wilder, troutman, fleetwood and all the ungendered fraternal players

of southwest Ohio, are crucial to that terrible arc of funk and flesh of which impossible mothers speak with

electromagnetic slide. Later, charged with the blackness of physics, its extralegal social surrealities, in search of

conceptual thaw having survived the river's violent floes and squalls, its seizing distancing, but drawn to the river of rivers of rivers, Lemon began a long series of residencies in itinerance. His efforts, filed under

vanishing in binding, disappear in the world's most important collections and divisions.

Our clearing is patrolled as a series of air, spirals in conjunction made by pointed running. It was affirmation

where we learned how to talk by walking pointedly, to organize air offstride by tapping, like a lion. My touch, my mouth all fixed to say these words, my listening in winter, my mirror glancing. Big-eyed cartoon, all this in

there as an audible surface that my eye wants to help you think about as you feel me. Feel me? That's why I always ask you if you feel me. Because I know you feel me. I ask you if you feel me because I know you feel me.

Another alignment of questions and I could be having a coke with you. I could be riding around with you, like

elements in an open field, spinning in ourselves till our supports collapse into a choir, a *batterie* of iron on the floor, a pallet on the floor, a plywood blanket for some intimate unrest. All these layers of not returning to

before and before, here come here come here come, are flowers made of crystal and crusted syrup. Our

seasoning is hambone and our self-abuse our swirling coattails and chant array. Big-legged cartoon, perform

our box of wonders from the book of wonder.

This order winds its way around the hills out from Oxford. Everybody fell in love with everybody hollering,

everybody waiting on everybody whining, everybody tapping and wobbling, the kettle whining, everybody

struggling to play, everybody staying while everybody come and go. We couldn't wait for labor day in Othar's bright-edged fusillade and savor. We couldn't wait without remembering them buried all together, Folosade

Thomas echoing and leading, winding at the head of our wailing abbey's forming with pleasure in abandon, tarrying, tasting in abandonment in stepping and studying why we can't.

Gone nowhere, gone everywhere, here come marching. This burled expanse of welcome homelessness sound

like marching. Here come here come last time. I sat and waited for you to leave. Ain't I gon' see you no more?
How can you stay? The southern question of travel makes a joyful noise and moves slowly in awareness. Now

we can speculate on the relay of our common activity, make a circle round our errant roots. Dancing is what

we make of falling. Music is what we make of music's absence, the real presence making music underneath.
I'm exhausted so my soul is rested.

Ralph Lemon was born in Alternative, Mississippi. Like many alternatives of Mississippi he was schooled in a chain of monastic launchpads, reading underconceptual repair, making arrangements and the theory of

repercussion. In repose in the experiment, set at an angle, just a-pausin' while a-sittin' and a-rockin', just posed

against standing, still inclined to engage in forensic study of the auction block of ideas and its stained wood but open also to her echo, his efflorescence, nothing—what else can you expect from corrosion in bloom?

corrosion in bloom is all you can expect; all you can expect is everything—is hard enough to enjoy.

nothing, even more, and another.

your things invite me so

quietly, I thought your

legs were so beautifully
shaven, your space was

light and different and

your surfaces, and your

brush, your application

is a movie with so many

sequels, such multiple

indemnities and hsian

potentials burn, nothing
even more and another.

aj, this for underneath your beautiful proof of concept.

Man, it is   but   it ain't fold or

                                   fold in or lay out or spin or walk awayarray

arrange. frere   keep
fading   aanic tape and flash and shit and broken stream

I thought was streamed with broken

rhythm where we went awry   are

we a broken category?

                                                   lull between pings but no

hard

inside pulse and more than

open enough   to not get bothered or to stand being bothered by overlap or by

                                     somebody watching or by

                               somebody else

but if it is

                               somebody else   or if he

                         is

                               here   this could be her

                               sound.

eve is a texture dave is centering.

eve is a texture

dave is centering
our whirring be

your bird ok

in government

and binding

nothingness is

in capacity

a moisture

unsurrounds
our gathering

and pouring

our came and

sent our drop

of chocolate of

a song in hand

our open bowl in
studio in assyrian
air in oil in serenade

interrogate our leaves
and air in saying

savoring of air

in stir from talk

of searing and

enhanced to hand

our salad is your

touch extreme

and braided fingers
dressed in sugar

through emulsion
like a spur your

final plural curve

mudede waters like josé muñificent.

the ordinary groove is strange. my accent be off

like that. the fremde, friend, is an ordinary fray.

you the from thing. shake your grove thing till
we're reunited at the angels' library. an annual

fade announced off fenian fenelonian fanonian

tranche but also that flange and quequenian la

as a rainbow of saints. my legacy is elegant but

found. aw, just appreciate/the little things I do.
the unusual threads and thrends are like doves.

are you every day and I really do love you every

day for a long time in another tongue? curving

is expecting you and we been studying the city

for a long time in our way of walking away with
the cutaway chute and coat and chassis by hand.

wait for it

you remain the future in our present like an accent pause that gramsci had to measure. living better now that double tap stop till then till that is your time we're in love with waiting. we can't so we can surprise so we can

attend and take urgent care. the erotic cure, which shows up as, which gives us, so that it ought to give us,

pause is our propulsion. who do what's been done can't wait for it and can't walk off. who recognize the

future don't wait on us, but because they don't know about service, about what it is to be an instrument,

decide they just ain't gon' wait. they miss something, they missing something, our liveness in reverb, this re:

that we refer to something, that we regard something, that we in regard to something else. they tell us what they think they know and we wait till they understand. I'm tired of waiting till they understand. see you later.

the gramsci monument

if the projects become a project from outside
then the projects been a project forever. held

in the projects we the project they stole. we steal

the project back and try to give it back to them.

come on, come get some of this project. we protect

the project with our open hands. the architect is in mining
and we dispossess him. we protect the project by handing.

let's bust the project up. let's love the project. can the

projects be loved? we love the projects. let's move
the projects. we project the projects. I'm just
projecting the project's mine to give away. I'm not
mine when I dispossess me I'm just a projection.

projection's just us that's who we are that's who

we be. we always be projecting. that's all we have.
we project the outside that's inside us. we the

outside that violates our block. we violate the auction block

experiment. we pirates of ourselves and others. we the friend

of all. we the cargo. are you my treasure? you all
I need. are you my wish? come be my sunship. you are

my starship. you meant to fly but don't be late. I dream

the sails of the project from the eastern shore. plywood sails
the city island past the enclave mirror till the bricks arise.

at the fugitive bar and the food be tasting good. kitchenette

my cabin and flesh be burning in the hold. I love the way

you smell. your cry enjoys me. let me taste the way you think.

let's do this one more time while the project repeats me. the project

incompletes me. I am replete with the project. your difference
folds me in your arms, my oracle with sweets, be my

confection engine. hear my plea. tell me how to choose.
tell me how to choose the project I have chosen. are you

the projects I have chosen? you are the project I choose.

all topological last friday evening

taken to bridges from lula to lela to lena to eula to ayler to tala to tore up
but untorn and bend

like fenders breathe, felder's or fielder's, that family, man, that recess.

so much more than air and world and time.
the general strike is that baby on your hip. your hip is radically pretending. we say I'm hep to that,

off sacrament. that unspeakable wish is a part of prayer, that edge so double

it's round, fray's embrace, which we breathe to make our song impossible to sing and not to sing.
check it out, now; you need to understand what I'm saying. it's a circular

saw in mr. johnson's thoat. his lungs are tender. this is a matter

of landscape, of *bildung* and arrest, and we laughed a long time

all

this complex word is an experiment. *All.* in her nocturnal upon hiring-day, being the hardest day, she

experiment like a scientist. she escape when she finish. I prepare you for the incline. the dancers were dodging

bullets but I love you secretly. the one I call to speak for me don't say. all green as virgil's moan, as jah's row, as

point's coup, my reasons turn your snows to green, what sass sound like in sarah vaughan. is wittgenstein silent

on love or just muted? is citation a mute or a microphone or miles' whisper muted in the microphone? it's all

asymmetry—gesture, small indenture, touch brushed down all the fall is, all that fall, world but complex earth,

but I can see the midnight sun. law can't really get there with you, all an alamillo of the so to speak. my

beautiful pylon, all raises the thing in hand absolutely. we gathered all our little alls, our little nothings, and at

our sailing he had brought his little all for a venture, on a stylus. the word presumes this interplay of excess and
poverty. you think you can veer and all turns native.

all up on that t-shirt

A recessed turn suspended in slow weight rub and field like a canyon but so quiet that it's vast in my ear on your hand, the mobile auditore and percaressive fan, in articulate faint and little spanfalls in palestra, syncopic fold in care of your contemporary negligee, in delection and commission I imagine.

akomfrahgment

the praline of amusement and

my cliometric pearl can't call it,
curve unnumbered. you can't

ride that long, you can't turn

that far, that cold coming and
going in and out of snow. the
speed of our washing is blinding

and our devotion is laughing
without a name or song. This is

our music. we're many hymns

in love with one another

warring out of circle almost,
almost frozen, color become

shape, you put your coat on me.

dance warm

garnette dance warm in my head
like a sweater. he says one love is

uncountable and I feel him. one love

is counter to itself and more than
that. more than that, it's perfectly

itself in every version. we've been
ourselves so differently that all this

dancing stay ready for us to smile,

having smiled, you got me smiling,

(you caught me) smilin'   again

which no one thought could be our

warm arrangement is embarrassed
with all this beautiful war inside like

babies making grammarless babies.

sweet nancy wilson saved frank ramsey.

The burden is also a refrain. That runs through you. You get no credit

or you get bad credit. Nevertheless, we write ourselves a sound

check. The one we come come to cash is written for us, on our
account. When Fred Wesley asked George Clinton what kind of horn
arrangements he wanted, Clinton replied, "Something bad!!"

Nancy Wilson and Cannonball recorded two versions of "Save Your Love For Me."

They ride and bear the history

of voice and horn, arrangement and derangement. Derangement is something bad!!

Even our arrangements move in relation

to the troubled pleasures of the first instance,
that can be sung (through the singer,

through words or their turning).

What gives you the right to love black music, this irruption out of and into catastrophe?

How are you justified in claiming these pleasures, in their terribleness, between
the impossibility of redress and the marked-up, marked-down, brutally

inscribed, viciously discounted remains
of the ones who, in spite of every anheroic act of getting over, can't get over, forming the lost body

of our broken bridge?

Salim asked me what I liked about Cecil and I couldn't say. So now let me say something about what I want from Cecil's music or about the way that music tells me what I want. Can I get to that or do I need to get over that or are these motions of getting to and getting over connected, as in the second instance? She was saving something, too. A social desire for sexual desire, often disavowed, indexed now as waiting. The incalculable

combination of extravagance and thrift,

their tuning.

Cannonball's not there in the first version but

now, since "we don't never know how we gon' be acting,"

he moves in the joint's held arousal, blurred unison, vagrant

shift. She joins and sings over Nat's fills and he becomes something like, but on the other hand way more than, a little brother giggling from upstairs, cutting his displacement, amping up the sociality, bringing noise.

Speaking of noise, what about the damage that

comes from desire manifest as repeated play? Over and over again indexes unfulfillment in indulgence. Sometimes

I listen just for the trace of that obsession now that digital technique keeps faith with the cracks and pops of love.

Between love and saving,

love and waiting, love and
                              singing what can't

be sung or said; between
love and salvation—what it is
   continually to be saved by the music, continually to ask

 this of the music from way back and way up ahead,

                                        where desperation and desire cut each other up to put
                              something away, the content of what
can't be said in the scar of singing something, for something other than that.

Will the love that's held

in these intimations that we love
save itself for us? Will the social life that makes itself
                              wait for us? Will the future,

                    recorded live,

hold on for us? I'm sweet

          Nancy Wilson way past singing. I'm fabulously Cecil
          Taylor of the feel. It's her part I'm always trying to sing, though she's not singing.
          Move my fingers to the feel, even though he's not here, alive, angled, remote, accompanied.

They unconceal—pattern

poised in elusion like it's sposed to be. Variation spends
the theory of saving and can't be counted.
               Bring across the secret that trusts no words.
                         Saying something beyond saying, in the exile

of voice and horn, whistled

               though it can't be whistled, said in singing

          though it can't be said, said in leaving
singing, said in leaving

               it unsung, song of desire, safe from desire, saved in desire.

I lay with francis in the margin.

I lay with francis in the margin.

my plan without surrounding
was in tact. my shift was extra

vagrant. my grain was terrible

and in decision was immigrant

and trans, I'm just so sensitive

and flighty, but francis curls me

into violet cradling and reading

to prepare for bordering and a
burthen for my numbering into

violent edging. francis, who's so
careful in the sight of his mama,

in her recital of handing, in her

unsold morsels, keeps straight

to the ornament's advance, man.

his lists are like knives and his

tongues, oh my god, are sweet as

maths. we're like westerns in a

togetherness; viv richards is our
accident and unforeseen exam.

ra, your gignity our echo.

over
heard
in pitts
burgh
4.5.13

but it turn out that everybody be returning our calls.

we were talking at easter dinner, in a thai restaurant,
about our favorite coefficients. never found a solution
talking about the problem, abandoned to ourselves in

piracy, enemies to all our states and selves; but from the
moment we get traction to the moment we lose track

we study sharing like players study playing. playing just

to play transfections of repertoire as strategies and tactics

of sharing to the end of the world. can we share the end

of settling? can I misunderstand you again, man, out of
love for extra? the north star is what's happening now

so I'm listening to difference in the joy of being extra,
which is the problem of the centuries. listening in pan-

african pan, resorbed in all for you, original suffer head,
like a new series of famous flames on bridge street, this

gspianic sound and ex cathedran groove is the original 2!

grad grind, gentles, till the park is gone.

his hair was like furry lining brushed and see-through and he was pale, his pinkness had a descent in it, like he had warmed down,

but you could tell by the way he took up space, scared somebody would get him for all that careless bumping into people,

trained in expansion at an early age, his demands at the informational meeting were sharp and unchecked in

his mother's
bloom, with her metal hands,

while his father explained the proper use of the materials to the principal. maria and cesar and the theory of handcuffs,

asking for what they took 'cause it's hot as hell between the baguette, don't bring your own tamales, and the house of york.

the plan when we were surfing was to blow the school for children up with urge, kilombo over more than across, get us some

land, see el durm in the window, for a long time

jaki byard, *blues for smoke*

excerpts from european episode. the history of the soloist who is not one, of one in nothingness in cherry and

choir, of things in blossom in aperture, a stray horn through a crack in the wall, the narrows between the open

mouth of the wall, the decreasing permanence of the wall in open air, up under the gun tower, spilled in

pipespace, embalmed, little brother's barrel, little richard's upswept twirl, her platform, her impossible upper
room and rolling stone, her hammond and her smoke, which can't be shown,

but you weren't there before it woke you. the history of double life and after hours, hollis stump and

apollo stomp on early rising, a fury, locomotive organizing sculpture breaking tools, equipped amuse epuise

tore up in vapor, whose monolithic skin has many skins, worn different than itself and others, all disorganized

in being worn, that cube on the makeshift bandstand, just a circle on the floor, a little inside squabble, the

sound of love without a terminal, his tinny, tinkling breaking apart is right on time, strode rode off into off-

stride in freddy webster's mystery, a movement in a distillate, quickening they can't shoot out of us, putney
stem and holcomb step to that hole on that hill that's on top of the world,

where the particles are still on tour. the history of the slur is lovely, no voice without the common

slur of owing, big underwritten road in arkansas chicago, unowned in open recipe, a breath of string to savor,

lyonnaise, milanese, the merely culinary expression that moves between them, destitute in that same old place

that if you can't love who do you love, when the dissonance is free and you know why you left a secret in the
workshop, abandoned every time they say one more time, an encore of mingus' alternative fingers horace

parlan brings around as something missing, speaking, can't you feel what you can't hold if you can hear, the
missive skip in code, decarava's fade, as smoke, for blue, which can be shown.

aluminum baby. discovery troubles things. his murmurs bury things to uncover them. he makes things prettier

than everything. he misunderstands. he forms an association of things that look like this, moving critical as

this stiff flow, he's aluminum. an autist gives you flowers, with a sound on edge, and aroma moves you to the

jitney stand across from ventos. an engineer in a broken sentence in a thick surround in garner's air, and

aluminum, who been mixing shade all day, the one they say a brawler, in kansas city. it's a still out the corner of

your eye, on the edge of the other side, a flower with an urn inside, her eyes covered, her ears shut down,

thinking how to get across, in theory, in wind, like memphis minimal.

pete and thomas—tribute to ticklers. abelard and tallis are in love. they met at a rent party next to an airshaft and fell. they never go to sleep. they spann time like morton feldman. back to back they play the beast with two fronts. other stuff get held back but not this, which is most tough, too. that bad habit of playing patty fingers, riding around in strange habit and carriage, as if the old days had old days that harnessed chargers and tillers, all fucked up from working, smuggled around like a rhythm section. rhythm sections smuggle, generally, as part

of their duties. they're domestic in a foreign sense and if you don't believe me ask susie ibarra. it's all love, as

you know. what they don't forbid they overlook, which is worse, as you know you know. but one never knows

do one. all one can do is take care of the one who keep one's time off, fold out in the water.

spanish tinge no. 1. like maroon speed and iberian note blacking on the loosaphone, when ferdinand was thinking

of expansion, wondering where the surplus would come from, wondering what the surplus was, wary as all his

cups began to fade, the theory of itinerant note blacking and line worrying was celebrating a thousand years of
bursting from the writing of its practice like a star. it was already there as something else from someplace else

always. when it arrives, as the difference you always move to be, from someplace else always that you never

been, welcome it like a tight chemise dropped in a storefront on one two five. the venereal nation under our

feet won't even have kings for a day. the spanish quarter, the latin quarter, the french quarter, the mill quarters,
and the barrack yards.

the flight of the fly. servants of the hardest time are the next spring. this is my sky song. the books in my cell are

a jackson in your house. see how idle chat gathers around things, that wood 22 was chopping, his axe? miss

thing chat fragile kit shake. huw is rough. hew be soft with longing. paul in mining. the social life of things

beside themselves, laughing through alan lomax. a lot of times, just sitting around, people be talking about the work it comes from. a lot of times people be sitting around talking about how some people think it only comes

from sitting around. mosquito turned that just by tuning up across the river. hear all that endlessly beginning segue in c? sing it so the count come back clear in a flat array of rows. parchman's general intellect is a blues

for julius eastman. count off, basically. julius eastman is the countess of the blues.

blues for smoke. the velocity of waiting, which is right next to the philosophy of waiting, most famously articulated in a blues called why we can't wait. the ensemble of particulate articulation, between black and flew,

razing and cantwaite, all the way to court and spark and flynt, is still on tour. i's a slow train you can look at

from beside the track. see every car pulse, when repetition stumbles, off abstraction. the period is a

degenerative condition, a developmental disorder. it associates with loneliness for the multiple. sometimes

they grow and sometimes they just curl, then chill, till the next episode. her ashes are everything folded over us in the cold, for the exhausted to return, aw, for the new thing to come.

jaki's blues next. just calling, just lining out while they sell that flour. here come presence out of nowhere. the social hum of movement is the essence of it, "because that is Black Power, that is one of the elements, a sitting

down together to reason, to 'ground' as the Brothers say. we have to 'ground together,'" in a gully, in a dungle, in the jungle, on an oil drum, till some furniture moving everywhere. the ballad of the underground is our

orchard hill, our clyde woods, our way of shearing, the sound of residue in spacing, like a bare living room in

the morning air. when he ready to get up and do his thing, when he wants to get into it, man, it's paramilitary

theory. the good foot is a blues march. the screamers are lost in thought, to prepare the song they pare, like a next machine, man. marshall allen is so close you can hear his people drumming, "we are nowhere, here, we are

elsewhere, moving, doing it, you know, down" slow, sounding, diving, the shape we in.

diane's melody. an air for daughter number two is lovingly submitted as an intersection of rainbows. when elvin

was talking about a yellow cymbal, the way a teacher might hold your hand, holding your face between my hands,

and we name the colors we hear. the club must have been a haven for a family man, providing in the heavy air
an air. back off in the woods was full with the love of children, the terror of blues for children. how many

generations in that room above the club? how many stories whispered in the groove of storyville? all the little
babies wrapped up in the corner. the relation between next (episode, breath, string, world) and our long night's
festival is blue, the sound we make so we can see, that broken chroma at the end, daddy, play my song again.

one two five. jaki byard is a sociologist. he is concerned with the "evident incalculability in human action." if a pattern were to emerge it would only be in refits and restarts, "the sudden rise at a given tune" that keeps

withdrawing. his hesitation is a singularity that becomes our engine. our engine is that continual propulsive chant that can't be said alone. the history of the ones who go off by themselves to make us say it. make me say it again. make me say it again, girl. see, this slight dehiscence is what I mean. it's got to be there, at the

rendezvouz of all in need, so we can hold our preferential option. the tortured logic of our line and run keeps

that in reserve for us, if we want it, but it's hard to want, it's so violent and beautiful.

test

(A small, and still isolated, incident in New York shows what can happen if authentic authority in social relations has broken down to the point where it cannot work any longer even in its derivative, purely functional form. A minor mishap in the subway system—the doors on a train failed to operate—turned into a serious shutdown on the line lasting four hours and involving more than fifty thousand passengers, because when the transit authorities asked the passengers to leave the defective train, they simply refused.)

Hannah Arendt, *On Violence*

More than 50,000 subway riders were stranded in the tunnels of the IRT Seventh Avenue line last night after passengers on a defective train at 110th street refused to leave as instructed by Transit Authority employees.

According to the Transit Authority, the trouble began shortly after 5:30 p.m. when the doors on a northbound train failed to operate correctly at 110th Street and Lenox Avenue.

One man said he had stayed in the tunnel directing others to the exits at 103rd Street. "I acted as though I knew what I was doing," he said, "because people usually believe you when you do."

Robert D. McFadden, *The New York Times*, January 4, 1969

this is how we never arrive, infuse what we surround to not remember. every day we cross from slave state to slave state in the barrack cars. we pass by, to avoid examination, in the sun. we were dark to ourselves when that bird start whistling in the tunnel. making music we were made to follow, fail to legislate, wouldn't get off got off so hard we got off everywhere. our breathing empties the air with fullness and we're in love in a state

of constant sorrow. the outcome is another process, a way into no way. the refuge is open and can't be safe.

the mobile engineer put some alternate dutchman pressure on. f train stand for fuck whoever won't ride.

the private investor's inability to afford himself is more and more clear as a general costliness. m2 just gone whenever they want to. people need to get to church and it's a bike tour. you can't drink that store-bought

coffee from a flying saucer. the animachine is henry dumas stopping bullets, wide-intervalled woody shaw flying transfers almost all the way to mermaid, the newly born instrument as a whole bunch of differences.

your refusal ain't unsustainable it just can't sustain itself. you do what they say till you die like a dog. too much

stress on the impossible one. we stress this past the point to bring the history of getting down. experimental

slant can't help but hurt you. look how hard and sharp it makes you breathe. you have to refuse in real time
with things that revise in real time when the wind is closed. there some ways not to love refreshment but they

all fucked up. we quiver with work and revival. we carry ourselves till you ready to hear what that sound like.

across 110th street is a helluva tester. the blackness of the witty partition be hand to mouth to hand and the

subway out of breath is an airshaft under a rent party. the rent party is the curriculum of the rent party

department. the department was so outlandish and groundless that she was arrogant for cause, stiff up in the

face of the unadmitted, as they exist on paper, in donation, in contempt of their training, though a citizen of

riverside, just up from hamsterdam, might not want to try to understand charisma. like kenneth warren, she

didn't know what african american literature was. soul courses in marburg were an expense of spirit in a waste
of shame. seelen were solo unadmittted, anechology of the supplement department, the burnt fringe of
speakers, la coping strada, bottom and jug off centering. everything, every good, every trumpet was deported

by her voice, which was never more than enough from holding her breath on riverside, where you can still feel
the burn of the eastern question, eastern man alone in her caress, feenin rubbed study in the desert, in the

church of the unnaturals, there's a riot going on and on for the making of black revolutionary stone on stone.

laura (made me listen to

1988, 2014,

daydream

and halting
made me

look at

music.

I started.

she was sleeping.
I started painting.

though nfrtt

the beautiful -1

has come.

though shrtr
in corona

language.

though

now and then in

air in

ease

in

interest
ed in
falling

through.
the little

edges

old women with babies and windows

show me that curving violet today.

it's fall across the park.

a doll baby, in the plaid

shirttail of los angeles,

held like a breeze

down the grass, a painting

running a nail's edge, barely

steel on a picture of forests on

a black flower, a steel bar tracing
black crossing on a violent swing.

the absence of your letter

shines.

taija the lonely weaver
veils wind around a spear.

the tree's mail sounds

like aspen. the chains

shine valdez. laila
the lonely colorist

is nia's velvet découverte.
immediately shade

be playing daydream looking

through.

thrill the air with a

regular flash.
        somebody playing

daydream looking through.

all the sun in colored

glass to play the mystical
        body. come and lay your

                come and brush

murmur garden.

brush with them

long rush by water.

lay tongues with 'em.

watch the langue

grow feline. in the

lagos and the vegas
spring and hush
inside. your form

is bend and form.

blow pretty behind

joe. never be the one

in sequence. of the flew
who work off collage

lil is following. Only

joe lies stone and dan
is stiffly breathing.

that slight stiffening

of paolo reading. as
amelita reading too.

silk

is

blue flying

around a relique.   you're a brush

but no soft delight

just hard delight
just curl talking
just urge talking

                              scr

                    atc

                                        h ang
                              el

like

johnny griffin.

in the light up close and black

and black in quiet parallel.

remember the recording angel?

kinda crack that window open, sweet.
through the sun, but way down on the tapestry.

delle bolton, elvin jones,
amalle dublon, johnny griffin

it's a funny old sort of day.
                    it's a funny old kinda day.
                                there's no

                    world.
                                selflessn

                                ess, an organ
                                waiting
            happily.   the day
            swings.
            holding, we hand and watch the
                water.
somebody lost, too, soft, too, the first
                november

                                lacing.

after twelve
I'm worse

than a gremlin.

I turn skin soft.

turn your lips soft.

soft water.

apricocks and
peaches.

we built some

cities. you are my

starship.
you
always hold
the
perfect ones. the
delicate
ones.
so
savage
in your

inner room.

left there, tied tongued, two'd,
your logic has a xhosan click

and we are softened.

what I learned

about the sonnet and you,
        wishing in these last few words

        between then and now, laura,

marlena shaw, and then and now
        are tremors,

        listening to touches,

the little edges   of occasion,
        at the heart of all occasions

acknowledgments

Versions of some of these poems
    appeared in *30 x Lace, American
    Quarterly, Finery: An Online Journal
    from Birds of Lace*, *Pen America*,
    Ploughshares, and *Social Text*.
"jaki byard, *blues for smoke*" appeared in
    Bennett Simpson, ed. *Blues for Smoke*
    (2012).
"hard enough to enjoy" was printed,
    along with images by Ralph Lemon, in
    a collectible volume by the Museum of
    Modern Art in 2012.
"hand up to your ear" was printed
    in a collectible pamphlet, *What is
    the Sound of Freedom?* by Ultra-red,
    in conjunction with Arika, for the
    Whitney Biennial, 2012.

about the author

Fred Moten is the author of
Arkansas (2000), *Poems* (with Jim Behrle;
2002), *In the Break: The Aesthetics of
the Black Radical Tradition* (2003),
I ran from it but was still in it (2007),
Hughson's Tavern (2008), and *B Jenkins*
(2010). He is professor of English at
University of California Riverside.

*A reader's companion to this volume is
available at fredmoten.site.wesleyan.edu.*